S0-BUI-594

THE LIGHT IN OUR HOUSES

Al Maginnes

The Light in Our Houses

Lena-Miles Wever Todd Poetry Series
Pleiades Press
WARRENSBURG, MISSOURI
& ROCK HILL, SOUTH CAROLINA

Copyright © 2000 by Al Maginnes

ISBN 0-8071-2622-5

Published by Pleiades Press

Department of English & Philosophy
Central Missouri State University
Warrensburg, Missouri 64093
&
Department of English
Winthrop University
Rock Hill, South Carolina 29733

The following poems were published in journals. My thanks to their editors:

Bellingham Review: "Currency of Where We've Been"
Brilliant Corners: "Between Tunes," "Elegy With Clifford Brown Playing
    Trumpet"
Crab Orchard Review: "The Lost Child"
Crazyhorse: "Cropdusters"
Defined Providence: "The Language of Birds"
Green Mountains Review: "Ghost Fleet," "Wild Dogs"
Greensboro Review: "Crossroads"
Half Tones to Jubilee: "Winter Ocean: Immersion"
Mid-American Review: "July"
North Carolina Literary Review: "Chasing Johnny Armstrong"
New England Review: "The Names of History"
New Orleans Review: "The Marriage of Clothes"
News & Observer (Raleigh, N.C.): "The Goat Man"
Poem: "The Other Side of Sleep"
Shenandoah: "Dancing Alone," "Punishment"
Southern Poetry Review: "Shades"
Tar River Poetry: "The Challenge," "Happy Endings"
Texas Review: "Lent"
Third Coast: "Renovation"

Cover image: "Moonlight, High Meadows, Andrus Farm," © Peter Poskas,
Schmidt-Bingham Gallery. 41 East 57th Street, New York, NY 10022.

Text designed & composed by Moreland Hogan, Charlotte, NC

Printed & bound by Thomson-Shore, Inc., Dexter, MI

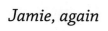

Jamie, again

Contents

PART ONE

The Marriage of Clothes 11

The Names of History 13

Punishment 14

The Challenge 16

Orphan Trains 18

Crossroads 20

Elegy With Clifford Brown

Playing Trumpet 22

Completion 24

Between Tunes 25

The Currency of Where We've Been 26

Dancing Alone 28

PART TWO

The Lost Child 31

The Goat Man 33

Invisible Stars 35

Chasing Johnny Armstrong 37

July 41

Crop Dusters 43

The Room Below the River 45

PART THREE

Renovation 49

Wild Dogs 51

Ghost Fleet 53

Winter Ocean: Immersion 55

Shades 57

PART FOUR

CALLING IT HOME   61

LENT   62

PRACTICING LOVE   64

FIREWORKS   65

WHAT WE WILL NOT DROWN IN   67

AFTER WEATHER   68

THE OTHER SIDE OF SLEEP   69

THE LANGUAGE OF BIRDS   70

HAPPY ENDINGS   72

PART ONE

THE MARRIAGE OF CLOTHES

There is a story, whose truth I don't know,
of a man who escaped from a chain gang
and changed his prison fatigues for a pair
of overalls hung on a farmer's clothesline.
The next morning the farmer found his pants gone
and dressed himself in the dew-wet prison clothes
that lay there and went to work. Before noon,
a posse discovered him splitting wood
behind his house and hauled him to prison
to finish the sentence of the man who stole
his overalls. When his time was done,
he walked home in the prison clothes that got him
arrested in the first place. His wife was gone,
the house a yawn of empty rooms, the fields
a long neglect of brambles and weeds.
The farmer walked out back and found his axe
still lying where it fell when the posse
grabbed him. He set a slab of wood on the block,
found the old habit of chopping once more.

If it ended there, the story would wrap
into some neatly folded Zen parable
about suffering and acceptance. But
this story, like most stories, does not
happen alone. The escaped prisoner
kept going until he came to a town
where he exchanged the farmer's overalls
for a factory worker's clothes. In these,
he traveled to a city where he stole
a banker's suit from a laundry truck.
Decently dressed, he found a position
in a dry goods store where he marked time
among bolts of patterned cloth, shoes made to fit
no human foot, jars of dusty candy
and coffee beans, dreaming of the suits
he would buy the afternoon he got paid.

And when a woman with the silence
of great distances about her walked in—
the woman most readers guess right away
is the wife of the farmer doing the time
that belongs to the man behind the counter—
he unravels bright tongues of cloth for her,
untangles snarls of ribbon, preamble
to their inevitable marriage of clothes.
The wedding night undressing, desired
and undelivered as the farmer's final axe blow,
lets the story continue, ignorant of
or ignoring our need for conclusions,
the gaudy clothes we wrap narratives in,
wearable emblems of our finite selves
and the infinite stories that go on
being told for the love of their telling.

THE NAMES OF HISTORY

When the first speared masts stabbed
a horizon where nothing had been seen before,
the shore-fishers turned and ran
for the dim embrace of trees, unaware
their steps were the first erasure
of the legends grandfathers had whispered
to quiet them on rainy nights.
From the pitching ship decks,
sailors eyed the rock-baited shore,
the sparse dunes, felt the teeth
loosening in their scurvid gums,
lowered a skiff into the water
to claim new land for their gout-ridden king.
 I learned early the hymn of plow breaking earth,
brick ovens rising and the first steel knives,
the songs of civilization we follow,
wherever they may lead us.
Yet what we have named history
was once only the braided rivers
of people's lives, currents that brimmed
fast and dangerous, then emptied
into the wide blank spill of ocean.

PUNISHMENT

When William Byrd arrived
at his lodgings late and found
the door locked, his servant gone to bed,
he recorded in his journal
that he woke the man and beat him.
Byrd neglected his prayers that night
but noted that he enjoyed
"good health, good humor &
good thoughts, thank God Almighty."

Almost three centuries later, my student slams
her hand like a joyous gavel
on her book, declares any man
who beats his servants unfit to read.
Each generation sees all that came before
reduced, the way things seen
through the wrong end of a telescope
shrink beyond our view. When my father told me
that he and my mother did not sleep together
until their wedding night, my laughter
must have struck him like a fist.

How do we defend old sins
except to say it was done that way
then? I wince when I recall
my response to my father, a kind man
attempting what guidance he could.
For years I could not give
my family's dinner-table talk a rest
as I put the whip to war,
racism, poverty, all the evils I considered
my parents the sleeping disciples of.

One day I will be lifted
from my own long drowse to learn
the banality of all my good intentions.
And when the blows fall on my back,

punishment for being a lazy servant,
won't it feel good to be the one
lifting the lash, convinced
of the justice in each blow?

THE CHALLENGE

Not my first trip down that road diving
and twisting off the blacktop. But this was night,
so I couldn't see the thundercloud of dust
our tires broiled. One of these tarpaper-sided houses
was where my mother picked up and dropped off Lee Ann
who twice a week cleaned our house and watched my sister and me.
Tonight my father drove. In the front seat stretched a silence
longer than the few miles between our house and hers.

On the back seat beside me rested a box of toys
my parents had decided my sister and I no longer needed.
When I rode here in the daytime, I leaned
into the front seat to watch Lee Ann's chickens,
dirty feather-clouds, cluck and scatter. One day
the summer before, her neighbor stood from chopping weeds
to mop silver sweat-gleam from his face,
and I asked, *How do black people get to be black?*

They're born that way. My mother hushed me
more quickly than Lee Ann shut her front door,
offering no glimpse of her life down here.
When my mother tried the next day to explain the difference
between races, I was simply relieved to learn
I couldn't turn black the way Mr. Bryan had teased I would
if I spent any more time in the sun.
My father stopped the car in front of Lee Ann's house.

We'd never parked before. Usually the pale dust
of our arrival barely settled, falling motes whirling
in dense sun, before the car made its pivot
and churned out again. But my father picked up
the box of toys, followed Lee Ann across
her moon-washed yard. I walked silent in their wake.
Few details of that room I'd stretched to see into
return now. The man and two women

in the front room went silent at our entrance,
their talk strained to polite, uneasy smiles.
Then the children, two girls and a boy my age,
appeared from the back hall, rubbing their eyes,
clinging to the sleep dark they, half-dressed,
had walked out of. Their eyes fumbled
from the box on the floor to me and back.
I could have tried to initiate them

into the best use of each toy, showed them
how to repair the airplane's wing when it fell off,
to substitute pennies for missing game pieces.
But facing each other across quiet deeper than child-shyness,
our silence carved one more chapter
into our inherited history of silence.
The boy finally spoke, answering Lee Ann's attempts
to coax a thank you. *I can whip you,* he said

so quietly it had to be true. When my father laughed,
the other man dared a dawn-slow smile. Lee Ann's son, encouraged,
slapped the air until his mother's single warning
froze him. This was Alabama in 1963,
still no place for anyone black, no matter
how young, to challenge anyone white.
When we left, my father's headlights cast
all that lay before us in bold, white relief,

the rest dropping into shadows too thick
to see the end of. I have traveled some distance
from that place, yet in the child-time that knows
only present-tense, I will always be there, the challenge
I cannot answer still in front of me.
And his raised hand, palm-flesh so close to mine in shade,
still maps the shared condition sun cannot bleach or burn away,
this thing we have still not thrown away or outgrown.

ORPHAN TRAINS

The half-moon arc of haunch, a feral slink
in her shoulders makes us wonder if she will ever
live easy among us, the puppy we picked up
from the roadside. A break in the brown
grass, one flicker of motion in all
that winter-dead color brought our eyes to her.

We believed when we brought her home, bedded her
on old towels, fed her food stirred soft in water
her unexpected lunges toward the wild would stop.
But a moon-roughed growl still strikes
flint in her throat, her fur rises like flame.
The families who lined up at train stations

or crowded prairie town churches to consider
the crop of orphans bundled onto trains
and shipped west by the Children's Aid Society
must have believed they knew what to expect.
Surely they who had brought crops out of scorch and drought
could coax these hard-seed children into families.

The untouchable distances children hoard
would only reveal themselves gradually. If big Jake Aberle,
who just wanted to adopt a boy, found
his new son staring away from some task,
how could he believe the boy's eyes were locked
on far-away city lanes, hallways whose stink

of urine and unwashed flesh refused entrance
to all but the most desperate? And if Jake fathomed
that dreaming look, he would not have believed
it was longing he divined in the boy's eyes.
But home is always the first place we know.
We can't blame the dog for the small, untamed place

she inhabits when our voices and hands
reach too close. She can't know
that her unplanned arrival only seems real

when we touch her, or how our hands stall
over other decisions. One boy who refused
two adoptions by farmers who treated

the boys they chose like unpaid laborers
found himself taken in by a childless couple
who had had no plans at all to adopt.
Because of this lucky stroke, the boy noted years later,
his life was a happy one. But most of the time,
cast out of one life into another,

we find even the old horrors a kindness.
So orphans dreamed of bedding down in alleys.
And the puppy, fed and freshly bathed,
growls from high grass where she hides
on her evening walk. And we, who a month ago
did not imagine her, crouch and sing her name,

coaxing her, this featherweight engine
whose walks and hungers are suddenly the timetable
of our days. Last month, our friend took custody
of her sister's child, and we wondered
if we could ever shoulder that burden of need.
This morning while the puppy circled our feet,

as if one filled absence creates another void,
we spoke of the child we do not have but might choose to have
until we chose to say no more. But the farmer
who fixed an arms across the shoulders of a boy
he'd only seen an hour before, the woman who took
a silent girl's hand to lead her to a new home

knew better than we what emptiness stands in the center
of any life and how little choice we have
about what we are given to fill it.

CROSSROADS

East of here, each crossroads wears a name,
so even those who live between towns
might say a place and be located.
And those hard, twanging names—Killquick,
Blackjack, Frog Level—sing a tune
as alluring and forbidding as the music—
watery harmonica, big-booted drums—
you might hear at night across a field,
blue light burning in the distance.

No one has ever said the name of the crossroads
where Robert Johnson was whispered
to have met the devil. But it might have been
on a night like this one, when a lunar eclipse
draws us outside to watch earth's shadow move,
graceful as a bedroom curtain falling, across the moon,
one more mystery cast by distance.

It's hard to stand under some change,
however brief, in the choreography of the heavens
and not feel yourself on the brink
of a turning both welcomed and feared.
When the name of each new town throbbed
like a secret, I hoarded those places
the way a guitar player gathers riffs and chords,
waiting for the instrument to let fly
all that lies just beyond his fingers.

Each crossroads bears its own landmark—
tiny store, post office, white-board church.
I believe the crossroads where Robert Johnson waited
was bare but for a lightning-scarred oak.
And when he left at dawn, he knew music
that kept young children awake at night
listening for the devil's footfall on the porch,
that kept their mothers fussing the curtains,
looking to see if that guitar player might follow

his shadow down that moon-thrilled road.

I don't return to the crossroads I know
to learn music or to stay. And Robert Johnson
might have left his crossroads,
unhaunted, with only cold fingers and pants
soaked with dew. But he would always know
the way back. Some places we touch once
and know forever, others take a lifetime
of burrowing in and building. And some we love
for the fine music of their names
and the way they turned us once
under the moon and sent us in a direction
we never believed we could go.

Elegy With Clifford Brown
Playing Trumpet

after Larry Levis

In the mystery I'm reading, Clifford Brown
may or may not have left behind more music,
something worth speculating for those who love

as I do how the quick angles of his playing
sound new light on a tune's surface

the way sun finds new faces
in the quick-peaking roofs of waves.

For the last month I've been reading the elegies
Larry Levis left behind, searching through them
as if the words, the bone-white space

between words, harbored his death. Somewhere
in those laments for seasons, for ancient horses,
for a world that is filled, not emptied, by loss,

lurked the hand that will come one day to touch us,
perhaps when we are right in the middle of things,

& lead us into a puzzle of streets
that we only understand slowly we will not
find our way out of, although that matters

less & less as the blacktop buckles & thins
to cobblestones, then to dirt, as we walk out of our shoes
until we are walking on nothing & then

we are not walking at all & the way back
to all we have left undone is forgotten.

One person has already died in this novel
& others probably will, falling in the unremarkable way

characters die in fiction—to further some plot need
or because they have outlived whatever use
the author invented for them. Larry Levis once said

that when his first book was published he waited
to become famous & did not write for a year,
a necessary silence he outlasted.

More than once, in the throat of some dark arena,
riding the frenzied pulse of a rock and roll band,
I made myself believe that somehow

we would, player & listener, outlast silence,
the moment's fever suspended & stretched
drum-head tight, the body held fast inside

the skin of the minute. But the band always stopped.
House lights came up like a dirty imitation sun
across a quiet so deep & sudden it seemed like deafness,

the audience one-minded & numb, shuffling to the exits,
leaving behind blankets, wine bottles, every brand of litter.

And there were always two teenaged girls
from a town three hours away, abandoned by their rides,
& one could not stop crying long enough to say her name.

Walking our new dog this afternoon, I watched her chase
the ink-black birds that gather on the sun-painted hill
behind my house. They scattered in quick distorted flight,

notes from one of God's unwritten solos.
I watched the dog chase first the birds, then their absence,

reminiscent of how we chase the dead, trying at last
to pin them down, as if their lack of motion

might halt our confusion. As day has burned
to its cold end, as my hand has chased
the quick-flying birds of my intention down the page,

I've been listening to the recordings of the Max Roach-
Clifford Brown bands of the fifties. I'm going to listen
to the tunes Clifford Brown recorded the night before

the car crash that killed him, then silence,
the place every note of music, every word,

even this one, finally falls down to.

COMPLETION

Bill Evans recording "Love Theme from 'Spartacus'"

Now, need for the drug, a timekeeper
more accurate and unforgiving
than music, trembles his fingers.
But music is still the greater need,
the palsied hands, the dope-sweat
rivering his back swept
under the carpet of notes
that must lie down more effortlessly
that even breath comes to him now.
In a few weeks, the tiny sword
of a syringe will nick a nerve
in his right arm, leaving him
to play a week at the Vanguard
with only his left hand and pedals.
A few weeks after that he will leave the city
to kill the hungry rat of his habit,
that incessant rodent gnawing
the bottom of his gut but never shaking
the internal clock that brings home
each track within a second of the one before it,
piano answering piano, the way hunger
feeds hunger, the conversation he cannot stop
having with himself—dope, music,
the sickness for dope all speaking
as he lays down the music
that a man alone in a room
more than thirty years after this night
will turn off the lights to listen to,
remembering the story from the studio:
Creed Taylor asking if he wants to stop
and fix. And the reply, through layers
of hunger, the reply a warrior might give
before battle: "No. Let's get it done."

Between Tunes

Nothing ended smooth in that loft,
each tune bumping to its rough halt,
then the voices: "What dragged me, man,
was my cigarette fell right in my drink."
And always one instrument teasing
that undefined space, searching some wisp
of melody, questioning saxophone,
stutter of drums, a raised voice:
"Drink it anyway." "I'll give it to you
and you drink it," before they stepped
slow and easy into one more tune.
This might have been the night
Eugene Smith captured himself,
camera raised, reflected
in the smooth bell of a saxophone.
This might have been one of the nights
that ended at the White Rose
nursing cheap beers, picking over the free lunch.
Or this might have been a night
that didn't shut down till long past dawn,
Zoot Sims chorus after chorus,
building on moonglow, stale puddles of oil
on tired streets, traffic lights blinking
their changes over empty intersections,
until they all walked out
into the raw daylight over the flower district,
perfume lifting from thousands
of trumpeting blooms. Upstairs,
Smith put his camera away,
rewound the tape that rolled
nearly unnoticed except for one who grinned
at Smith's need to get it all down
and called, "This one's for history, men,"
just before the music started again.

THE CURRENCY OF WHERE WE'VE BEEN

The first throttle of ink
under my skin was a relief,
the grinding ink gun
translating decision to action,
etching my flesh with the bird
I had long pondered wearing.
On the wall, a line drawing
of a schooner in full sail
distracted me, conjured
a sailor on the rear deck
watching the last slipping
of land below the horizon's lip.
Once the anchor has been weighed,
the sail opened, all that came before
makes a past as distant
as those on shore who still wave
farewell long after the ship is gone.
How would those who remain
understand the largest part of any journey
will be spent waiting for a wind
strong enough to bear the ship
beyond the horse latitudes
of indecision? It is out there
the crew spits sour hope and mutiny.
Birds brought signs of land
to Noah and Columbus, two captains
made legend by good fortune.
Because we must prove
the direction we travel in,
we seek talismans along the way.
Hence, the ocean-rounded stones,
the shells turning to grit
in the floorboard of my car.
Hence, the bird, burned,
mid-voyage, into my arm.

And hence, the inches of tarred rope,
the limp gull feather
my imagined sailor pocketed
when it seemed water would be
his voyage's unmarked end.
But he would return with tales
of black sand beaches, birds
with fire-bright plumes, women
dark-skinned and ornamented with ink.
Some nights around a hearth
or tavern table, he'd display
his hoard of shells, explaining
that where he'd been, these passed
for coins. And passed from hand
to curious hand, they glowed
fresh as new-minted dollars,
the currency of where we've been
as fiercely earned and unspendable
as anything we wear on our skin.

DANCING ALONE

One song crowds into another.
No choreography. Just tremor and feel.
Since partners and the old rites
of request and refusal are abandoned,
contact comes furious and accidental
out of the solitary thrash
that risks no silence.
We've surrendered Sunday drives,
the long memory of geography,
the radio off, one hand raised
to the locals, all of us pretending
we live in the same place,
pull the same mail from our boxes.
The girl in the leopard leotard
has read nothing for months,
believes evolution will move us
beyond our use for hands.
The message she gets is rhythm,
ringing her phone,
calling for more space
than our weave of bodies allows.
This is how we move
at the end of the American century,
ceaseless and alone, amnesiac
in the strobe of glitter and throb,
the grind that hammers us
toward the sky's open sutures,
the white flag dawn will raise.

PART TWO

THE LOST CHILD

Our Cub Scout troop followed a ragged single file
through damp shadows and ponds of light
on our field trip under Allatoona Dam.
We kicked each other's feet and laughed at nothing until,
at the edge of a cavern layered with metal catwalks,
routed with long pipes and shuddering machines,
our guide warned us not to stray outside the painted lines.
One boy, he said, wandered off and was never found.

When we camped out that night, I would close my eyes
and see nothing but that boy whose name no one would tell us,
edging away from his group, their echoing voices going dim
as he traced one pipe around a corner only to find it
coupled to another pipe, then one more,
until, when he was ready to go back,
there was only darkness and water somewhere dripping
ceaseless as a clock, and every direction might or might not
      lead him home.
Gary Fox leaned over, whispered, "We wouldn't get lost."

The lost boy still returns unpredictably, caught
in the drift-net of reverie, his age dwindling each year,
his flesh at once more ghostly and more real, his eyes luminous
      as lost coins.
A fading memory of light tugs him through that underworld
where pipes roar with captured water, gauges pivot with psi's.
The light bulbs popped dead long ago, leaving him
the same dark that fills the windows
that the parents of every lost child look out of,
praying the names they no longer say aloud.

I have no idea what has become of Gary Fox or any of that line
of boys under the dam. My family moved, then moved again;
those boys have gone wherever they have gone.
They surface attached to incident, faces struggling for names,
then slip back into the swift-moving water
whose one bank is forgetfulness, whose other is time.

The pent-up river above our heads,
we were told, let the lights in our houses burn.
And when I walked back into the bright rooms of my house,
I felt myself, for the first time, thrust on the tip of current
that pushes us where we are going too quickly to know how we got
    there.

THE GOAT MAN

Constructed as he seemed to be from words, generations
of rumor and terror laddered from child to child,
he might not have been there at all or simply unraveled
into morning fog at our approach. Instead,
he grew more solid, pot-bellied in patched overalls
and three shirts, his beard a tangled Old Testament mystery
he muttered through as he scattered feed
for his flock of fierce-eyed stinking goats.

Some said he was a defrocked preacher, too smitten
with God to be confined to Sundays
and Wednesday nights. Maybe if I'd watched
a while longer, I'd have found more to his faith
than cursing the world and wandering—
not the last time I'd encounter that combination
and one I'd try myself for a few seasons—
but the morning was cold, my father restless.
The goats pawed the wet dirt, chomped their feed
while the goat man swore at and cajoled them, ignoring
the handful of townfolk gathered around his herd
and his motley wagon while cars sang by on the highway.

Twenty five years later in a Tennessee novel,
I found a mad preacher driving a goat herd,
and that old man was resurrected
with his folders of printed prayers, his devil-eyed goats.
If it was him or some written shadow of him,
I don't know, but the fog that hugged
the Georgia clay that morning swirled
across the page, the first time I wondered
why a man given to God would choose goats,
would take for his family a four-legged
approximation of Satan. Why not drive mules,
closer kin to the lowly and more Biblical ass?

Every childhood has its totems, and he
was one of mine, a signpost back

to that town I could not stop dreaming my way out of
and dream my way back to now, looking
for the heart-shaped prints the goats scribbled
in soft mud beside the broad flat tracks
of his brogans, hieroglyph of one of the Lost Tribes
who vanished into the early dawn of fire
leaving no alphabet we could read
to say who they were, where they were going.

INVISIBLE STARS

The missing children live with us, a constellation
of class pictures ignored on milk cartons, on postcards
that ask, Have you seen me? The answer
is always no, the dates of disappearance
so improbably distant I can usually avoid
being delivered to an afternoon passed over
for more than a quarter-century. I must have been
coming home from the library or prowling
drugstores and five-and-dimes full of nothing
I had money to buy. I was eleven
or twelve; the world had yet to touch me
with the hard stubble my father scraped
from his face each morning. And what was there
to fear in Colonial Grocery's parking lot
four blocks from my house? How old was I?
he wanted to know. A gold ring glowered
on the hand that tapped the steering wheel,
making the noise of small bones clicking together.
He had some work he needed some boys for,
but I might be too young. Why didn't I get in,
show him where to find some boys big enough
for what he needed? Years of warnings died
with no whisper in the slam of his car door.
I shook my head at the cigarette he offered,
and we slipped into the thin traffic
of late Saturday afternoon. If I looked
at him more than once, I can't say,
recall little for memory's sketch artist
to color in now: thick arms,
a white shirt set with some arrowed pattern.
Oily hair arranged across a bald spot.
A man, plain as any other
who might ask directions in a strange town
or coach the other side in a Little League game.
On the radio, music I had not heard before

played reckless and fast, faded as he asked where
the boys in town hung around, asked names, ages.
His wide hand drummed the seat between us.
With every answer, I vanished,
nameless as any child never seen again.
None of the things that could have happened did.
I showed him the high school, the Hurricane drive-in,
things he must have already known.
And he must have sensed how much I did not know.
But as he steered me back to where he found me,
the streets I knew like breathing went strange
in the sigh of gloam-light
and the space between us filled
with my first inkling of what might wait
in a dark that hides the demands
of mouths, hands, other bodies.
Then I was in Colonial's parking lot,
held breath of twilight rising around me.
The sky emptied as I started home,
then filled with night and the first vague light
of a few lucky and foolish stars.

CHASING JOHNNY ARMSTRONG

1.

It could have been you. And it was
you I thought of when I heard the name
of the man who took two children

hostage in a trailer park in Florida.
He was about the right age, had your name,
and every description—let's say it was not you—

was vague, cooked through with phrases
like "career criminal" and "history of drug abuse,"
someone, in other words, who could be

safely shot down. Which is what happened.
And I kept remembering a day in gym class, eighth grade,
when you, barely breathing hard, outran

the whole class in the mile. A few months later,
your right leg was crushed in a car wreck.
After you came back to school, after

the cast came off, you still dressed out
for gym but sat in the bleachers, the purple
cross-hatched scar glowering on your leg

like a warning. And still, you knew
how to outrun us, growing your hair so long
you were threatened with expulsion, sneaking off

to concerts in Atlanta while the rest of us sweated
at dances where bad bands knocked out
covers of "Mustang Sally" and "Knock On Wood."

2.

For the two days the story took
to unravel, I kept returning to the papers,
to television, trying to get a glimpse

of the man who might have been you.
Last summer, driving through our town
I kept looking for a face I knew.

The junior high is closed now,
used for storage and locked tight
behind a chain-link fence topped

with a triple strand of barbed wire.
Even the windows are painted over,
as if to hold in the hundreds of hours

worn to dust there, the ten million
sighs that tried to erase
or speed the clock's unmoving hands.

It frightens me:
how little I remember of the time
I spent there and how little I like

of what I do remember.
What returns is always the slow limbo
of those years, fixed

against the fluid revisions of memory.
What is the past but a series
of locked windows we peer through,

hoping to sight a familiar piece
of furniture, the end of a story
whose beginning we know by heart,

the blood's old song pulling us back
even as we give thanks
for whatever distance the years grant us?

3.

It is the uncertainties of the body
that return, your shattered leg
a symbol, somehow, of what could happen,

the world we could not control. On the day
you came back to school, after weeks

in the hospital and at home, one

of your wild friends galloped your wheelchair
down the hall, your white cast thrust
before you like the figurehead of some tiny ship,

declaration of your intention
to slow for nothing. The last time I saw you
I was seventeen, visiting, surprised

to find the same changes
that had washed over me had visited
everyone else in my absence.

At a party full of faces I had once known,
I saw you strumming the air, miming
the work of the band's lead guitarist.

We said hello but little more.
It has taken me until now to remember
we were never friends.

4.

Whatever our lives do to us, they do it
so slowly we do not see it happening,
the way history is finally

one day coming after another.
Tonight you might be coming home
to a woman who loves you, children sprawled

before the TV in a clutter of toys.
Or you might be walking into an apartment
empty but for one ill-natured cat.

You could be speaking in tongues, shooting up,
entering conspiracy data into a computer.
Too many lives divide us

for me to guess. Next time I'm in that town,
I might search your name in the phone book,
but we both know names can outrun us,

end up in places our lives never dreamed.
If only a few things had been different
it might have been you, might have been me

chased breathless into that trailer,
an entire life hostage to the moment
when charge and surrender become the same.

5.

This is the life that keeps you
sleepless, wakes you in the grease
of your own sweat, your heart screaming

until you start to question memory.
And if you do not believe what you remember,
you must ask if you really know anything.

So I return to the place I began,
aging runner circling the track to find
a line of boys, legs flexing, necks tickled

with sweat as they wait
for go, the thunder of our feet
making the first step together

before speed separated us
into the noise each boy made
trying to outrun or catch up with the world.

JULY

The heat conspires to make us too aware
of our bodies. In high school, on nights like this,
we gathered on the curved roads
of unbuilt subdivisions or in parking lots,
beers going warm as quick as we opened them.
Once in a while, I see a name from those nights
in the cold print of the newspaper.
The news is bad more often than it is good.
Last week, just as this canopy of heat locked in
above us, one of that crew was caught
trying to torch his ex-mother-in-law's tool shed.

One night, mindless of the season, we built
a fire in the middle of an empty stretch of asphalt,
fed it windfall limbs until flames shot
higher than our heads. We ringed the fire,
moving back from the heat that would consume
all we fed it, leaving only
crumbled embers and a zero of ash.

And we would feed it anything.
Before the end of June, boredom burned so deep
we'd give ourselves to any risk we could survive.
When Scott Barlow died on his motorcycle,
when Billy Lin was shot or the warehouse burned down,
even the ones who weren't there memorized every detail
in order to tell the tales survivors tell.

But the night Hal Whitfield started one more fight
be could not win, I did not even leave my seat
on the fender of someone's car. Even after the knife
flashed its single exclamation point and left Hal
holding shut the jagged smile torn in his arm,
I only felt I'd seen this before.
Four years later, Hal Whitfield would blunder
into a couple's bedroom waving a shotgun,
looking for someone who no longer lived there.

I was gone by then. I know the young,
given entirely to the needs of the body, still gather
to taunt the humid air with their unscarred flesh.
I would not give back or live through one of those nights again.
They return anyway, an endless reel of memory
burning, revising my migration
into this body, this heavy, damp building
that burns down one slow day at a time.

CROP DUSTERS

No reserved seats so forty thousand of us funneled
through one gate running, a heedless lemming-rush
that carried us into the locked glass doors of the arena.
Pressed against the glass, we must have resembled
a multi-limbed, many-faced aquarium creature.
On the auditorium floor, the crowd thickened like smoke
while on the stage above us, roadies posed with their bosses'
    guitars,
and oxygen became a commodity more precious
than good seats or the cheap acid and angel dust that littered
the parking lot. When people began to fall like chopped weeds,
they were passed over the crowd's heads, a conveyor belt
of hands moving bodies forward even as we grumbled
over how long we had to stand for this.

But when the music swirled its dusty cape around us,
we were rabid acolytes, head-bobbing fodder,
ready to fall on our chemical swords. When machine-bred fog
rolled across the stage in waves, swallowing the players,
hiding the front rows, some paranoid minister in my brain
    expected
the band to emerge wearing gas masks.
My wife told me that she and her friends used to ride
their bikes behind the trucks that rolled
through Southern neighborhoods just before dusk,
shooting its white mist of mosquito-killing compound
into the air. The game was to be soaked by the fog.

Riding from one dry-wall job to another, my boss parked
on a back road one afternoon so we could watch
the tree-skimming acrobatics of a crop duster
at work, the rickety plane swooping low
to let a white dust of pesticide fall over the field
as neatly as a sheet drops over a mattress,
then lifting clean as a blade, the plane's metal belly
just missing power lines, the tips of black pines

before turning for another run. Years later,
a man sitting next to me in a bar told me
his father died when the wing of his crop-dusting plane
tipped a power line, sending the plane wobbling
into a line of trees across the road. The wreck burned
longer than anyone thought it would, he said,
safe inside the room bar whiskey had built for him,
a place where he would tell a stranger this tale.
He was sure it was the chemicals.

I still hear that band droning from the radio,
predictable as a motor. Jamie and I buy organic vegetables;
she will not use even bug spray to thwart
the persistent summer invasions of ants and shudders
to learn someone younger than she has cancer.
I still slow to watch crop dusters buzzing fields,
dropping their payload and finding an angle
that lifts them into clear sky, all blood aloft
in the keening, in the steel-feathered edge
my most extreme moments have found, when
my eyes and nostrils so filled with what swirled around me,
I believed what I was doing was worth my life.

THE ROOM BELOW THE RIVER

Every summer a few bridge divers disappear,
arc from the waist-high railing to break
some swift-muscled river's brown skin
and never come up. Some will be found
a few days, a week later, miles downriver.
The ones we remember are never found at all.

In one of my childhood books, a boy dived
to the bottom of the river to find a chamber
where some treasure needed for his journey home
was hidden. His return to the realm
of light and air was meant to be a rebirth,
but let's believe those boys who never surface

learn to outlast the need for air, are born
into some long-sleeping instinct that homes them down
to a room below the river's moveable surface
where they will never age, where their bodies,
 lost to the sun-ravaged world,
never surrender the tanned grace they found

in lifting from the rust-scrawled iron rail.
Let me not dwell on what befalls
a body submerged too long, on the appetites
of catfish and tooth-snouted gar, beings
fitted so perfectly to their existence
a thousand centuries have marked no change.

Because my family moved every year or two,
I taught myself no surface was permanent.
In each new room, I lined my books
on shelves, scattered treasures around me,
trying to build a room where things held still
against the changeable streams of roof and wall.

I needed to believe one structure could hold
iron-steady before I took my own dive
into the hold of hard-moving currents.

But a new world awaits every rising,
our old theologies shifting with our motions,
with our need to be submerged again.

From their room at the river's bottom,
the disappeared boys can spy up and see nothing
they want, not the slow rusting
of the bridge they stood on or the mobile
and aging surfaces their land-bound companions find
rippling in the clear water of mirrors.

But from those depths, they cannot fathom
the chamber locked in each human heart,
the place where we hold ourselves against time.
In that room, I am still the age of those boys
I passed on a bridge today, who turned from my gaze
to study the field of water below them.

I knew as soon as my dust settled,
the road once more an empty gulch,
they would launch themselves again,
bodies straining for flight, as if they knew
how much they would treasure this against
all the downward commands of gravity.

PART THREE

Renovation

In the stark noir of street light,
the house's exoskeleton of scaffolding
might be the house trying to crawl,
serpentine, out of its own body.
Shadows disappear inside the skin of paint
the owners are counting on to make
the shambling Victorian the house
they envisioned, the way a mother might
insist on a coat and tie to hide
her son's ashy and dirt-loving heart.
The carpenter's helper, who walked here
after dark to retrieve the tool belt
he left on the porch, stares from the sidewalk
at the cold smear of light
against the window's black panes,
a featureless series of white disks that reflect
no notion of what is being made new
behind the glass. Two nights ago,
two of the boxy, faceless houses
being raised in the new subdivision
near his house burned. He stood with his friends,
drinking beer and watching the twin fires howl,
until both houses huffed like tired lungs
and fell on themselves. Smoke still stained
the air yesterday morning. On this block,
the houses seem immune to fire
like women so gnarled with time
they are impervious to any calamity.
It's been a year since his grandmother's death
and his refusal to wear a tie to the funeral.
In that year he has left college and begun
trying to gather a handful of skills,
and, sometimes, in the swirl of sawdust
or the racket of hammers, he feels sheltered
from the ravages that strip houses

to helpless wood and cold rooms.
The night of the fire, he considered calling home,
but those arguments are narrow-doored rooms
treacherous with old furniture, places he needs
more light to negotiate. Each day
he learns more about reading the young wood
being used for this rebuilding,
how much will be cut, how much will be scrapped
and burned before the house rises
solid and recognizable out of its past.

WILD DOGS

Sometimes when the music's twist and churn
goes flat, when he sees his bandmates' eyes
tick to stone, their rhythm sagging
to the dreary mechanics of the worst fucking,
merely the act without joy or discovery,
                                             he retreats
inside the cone of sound to the summer
he was nine and wild dogs roamed the woods
at the end of his street. Like most things since,
the notion proved richer than the reality.
He dreamed sleek shadows, quick and just
across the nightscape, not the tribe
of yellow-fanged, fur-matted mutts
slinking feral and silent across the red mud
of a lot where a new house rose.
Warned away by parents, by neighbors,
he could not keep from trying to creep close,
imagining he might capture one and tame it,
coaxing out of it the thing he loved most.
But if he stepped too close,
a fence of warning growls raised,
teeth that had, he knew, torn the flesh
of cows, of cats and neighborhood dogs,
suddenly bared in his direction.
                                       His father leaned
with other men on the beds of pickup trucks,
counting in low voices through ways
to be rid of the dogs, fearing them
as anything once tame turned suddenly wild
is feared, ears newly tuned to voices
no domesticated hearing can fathom, the way
the boy's parents would puzzle in a few years
over the angles and colors of his hair,
the silver jewelry threaded through needle holes

in his body, the wall of noise he built
with his guitar to hide his silence.

The morning he walked outside and heard guns
ringing in the woods was the only time
he ever wished to be deaf.
                              In the post-din quiet
of clubs and concert halls, as equipment is torn down
and loaded out, a few gaunt, shiny-eyed listeners
always come out of the shadows, figures
shaped by noise, hoping for a few words, another song,
reaching for him even as their hands remain
fisted in their pockets, wanting from him
something rare and unsatisfying as the taste of blood.

GHOST FLEET

Hatteras, N.C.

In a shop filled with mounted sand dollars,
postcards and plastic pirate swords, they buy
a map that locates and names every craft
that ever went down off the Outer Banks.

Back in the car, he again rakes up
the story about the time he and a friend,
real dollar poor, dredging bottom muck for clams
uncovered a cache of sand dollars,

the only live ones he'd ever seen and these mating,
flat sides pressed together, the bristly hairs that covered
their bodies hooked so they made a tearing sound
coming apart. She's heard this story before,

but the recitation makes his voice a pleasant drum
against the rain and slow mist that conspire
sails of fog. High narrow beach houses loom
out of the murk like ships nameless and miles off course.

This morning, they woke and made love, then slept
to wake and make love again. Only a few weeks ago,
he left quiet as fog without saying why, steered
by the notion that his life had quietly blown off course.

Anchored by time, by habit, by all his story has no words for
he returned, hoping they had not become wreckage,
a vessel vanished so long ago only a name, a date remained
the way people are only names at first, faces

that give no hint of the rooms sealed behind them.
The map rolled in her lap reminds her
of her childhood nightmare of never being born,
of the life she knows going on without her

and no voice remarking her absence.
And his story, drifting to its familiar end, requires at least

her presence: he and his friend bleached the sand dollars
and tried to hawk them on the boardwalk,

a constellation arrayed across a dark towel.
They did not sell one. Walking home that night,
they set their harvest on cars, fence posts
in the middle of intersections. The largest one

he saved, threaded a nail through its hole
and hung it over his bed. It still hung, tiny moon,
over the bed he slept in when they first met.
The nights he was gone, her bad dreams

of absence returned, and she drove for hours,
avoiding the stale harbor of their house
to navigate streets she didn't know, to forget
how simple the act of coming apart can be,

how easily the best built craft becomes wreckage,
one more name the ghost fleet carries.

WINTER OCEAN: IMMERSION

There is no rest in the rain, a metronome
striding over the lifts and valleys
of the clock's sleepless minutes. Beside him,
she lies marooned on her side, one hand palming
her pregnant belly, her steady sleep a reproach
to his waking, to the winter of the Carolina coast
that seals them inside a badly-heated rental
on the last week of the year. At last,
he rises as he has known he would.
She stirs once and moves to the center of the bed.

In the near-painful light of the kitchen, his reflection,
an unborn twin, watches from the sliding glass door.
It was here, first week of May, shrimp butterflied
and broiled in butter, wine easing
the first sting of sun on winter-soft skin,
where they slid to the floor, looking up in mid-love
to see themselves doubled in the glass door
as though this time the act required more
than the two of them, their coupled motion a summons
to the small passenger who swims inside her now.
Outside, dark houses, stuffed with winter, hibernate.
He strips quickly and steps onto the deck.

Out here, no reflection, as if he has stepped
into the body of that shadow twin. The lit kitchen,
the book sprawled on the table beside the green mug
suggest totems of a life beyond his reach
since the December twenty years before when he
and his best friend Jeff, both home from college for Christmas,
hiking near a river, stripped and eased themselves
into the roil of brown water that burned their skins numb.
Grasping a shelf of rock, they held themselves
in the water until their blood matched the water's temperature.
He jogs off the deck, up the dark street
toward the still-unheard ocean. He and Jeff climbed

out of that water, back into their bodies, claiming
to feel reborn, and shivered all the way home.
A handful of years and his telephone would ring
to tell him that Jeff, his other half, the brother
he should have had, was dead, outrun, finally,
by a body that could not stop risking itself.

A far-off car horn reminds him how difficult
it will be to explain this if he is seen.
But it is important to reach the water,
to ignore the sharp gravel chewing his soles,
his body's complaints against the cold, if only to fulfill
his imagination of telling the unnamed child
about this, if only to prove he is a man not bound
by the small rules others fear, to outrun
his blood's reckless twin taunting him
with the risks he no longer assumes.
Colder than air, the water lures him in, promising
the warmth he recalls from that river, the joy
that howled out of him when that water first touched
his skin, when no twin, no ghost of deeds undone
lurked at the bottom of his life, breathing through all
he has used to smother it. Then he is underwater,
flailing, black tons of salt pushing him down
until, spitting for air, he crabs his way back to sand.

Some immersion, whether in the strange waters
of oceans and winter rivers, in the four-cornered
world of books, in the old swamp of booze and drugs,
in distance running, martial arts, exotic cookery,
must carry him deep enough to enter the body
of that perfect other life every life dreams of.
But in the breath-starved second before surfacing,
he only wanted what he has now:
the chance to jog back on numb legs, to dry
the cold baptism of ocean and rain,
to warm himself in the life he has
and sleep beside his wife, one man made whole.

SHADES

He did not know there was this much flour in the world.
All morning the boy shouldered fifty pound sacks,
walked the hot tunnel of the tractor trailer down the ramp
into the brief blast of sun, then the cool dark of storage
over and over, each trip unremarkable as breath.

By noon his bones were ground to powder as fine
as what sifted down his back, and he could have fallen
where he stood and chewed mute mouthfuls of flour.
But he followed Lenny, the bakery owner's jack-of-all-trades,
into the shade of three oaks and swallowed his dry sandwiches

while Lenny pillowed his head on one thick forearm
and slept, his slow breathing the only motion that betrayed life.
The boy traced the roads sweat had cut
through the flour dusting his upper body,
rolling sweat and flour into a blackened dough,

making raw biscuits of the body's labor until
Lenny woke and they left the shade. Years later in a lit class,
he learned that shade was another name for a ghost,
what was left of man after the body emptied.
Two years after the day they unloaded the flour,

Lenny was killed cutting firewood for the bakery owner
when the chainsaw blade leapt in his hands,
chewing into the soft meat of his neck until an artery split.
The boy did not make that funeral. But he did go
to the burial of the bakery owner, his father's friend,

who died hunched over a putt on the sixteenth green.
Near forty now, no longer a boy, he stands
in his new backyard, pacing off his garden plot
as carefully as he chose his father's gravesite last year,
making sure that the last property his father would claim

took the full stare of morning sun before the long
encroachment of shade men will only lie down in

if they know they will rise again. When he and Lenny went back to
       work
their arms and shoulders ghost-white with flour,
they could count the rest of that day in the sacks that remained.

No work he has done or will do outwits death,
but without work, life is dry bread, time slowly chewing itself
until the eyes close for the last time. He wants
the breaking of powdery dirt, the burial and springing forth.
He wants to be sure no shade falls where he stands.

PART FOUR

CALLING IT HOME

When we heard the couple describe
the zealous timing, the exhaustive
collaborations of their efforts to conceive,
our eyes met and moved away.
Acknowledging what? Our children
unborn? The long spaces
between our touching? Two summers ago,
to escape the listless heat of our house,
we drove a dirt road
where deer were known to emerge
like tan shadows out of the woods.
We parked in shade and waited
in haze of pine pollen and dust.
A small motion near the scorched field's
tree-line and a doe appeared,
followed by two fawns. They saw us and froze.
A long moment of wary regard.
Then you made with your tongue
a soft clicking sound
I have not heard from you before or since.
And slowly, improbably, the smallest fawn
moved toward us. One step,
two, it came closer until
some unworded signal arrowed
from bodies we tried to hold still as trees,
and the deer turned and ran
back into the womb-dark woods.
Beginning a new life must be like that.
Something small and wild moves
on the edge of your vision. You call it
and sometimes it comes close enough
you believe you can give it a name.

LENT

Because his wife called him a selfish son-of-a-bitch
before she slammed the car door and left,
and because his married girlfriend has given him up
for Lent, he's dyeing eggs in his kitchen
the night before Easter and contemplating
the notion of sacrifice. What is gained by living
without what you desire except the sharpening
of desire? Sacrifice swung its specter
over the church of his childhood, a censer
lading the air with an odor everyone called sweet
but no one wanted to live with for long.
When he was young enough that purity seemed possible,
he resolved each year to give up something
he was sure to fail at, like desserts, and to stuff
the mite box he got in Sunday school full.
The last year he tried, two friends told him
they were going to buy model cars, and suddenly
those shiny models tempted him more than he remembered
ever wanting anything. The mite box opened too easily,
coins and soft bills a satisfying knot
in his pocket. The model wound up half-built,
wobbly and glue-smeared, in back of his closet,
one more promise not kept. When the Sunday school students
delivered their offerings to the altar, he held his box very still
so the few coins he'd dropped back into it
would not ring against each other, silver tongues
hymning his doubled failure. Spooning out
the last egg, it occurs to him that his girlfriend's sacrifice
has become his as well, and while he itches for her
in a way he never has, he likes the notion
of being as tempting as cigarettes or chocolate,
more traditional renunciations. Tomorrow morning,
he'll drive forty miles to weather his wife's silence
and give his daughter a basket of candy and colored eggs
he'll say the Easter bunny left with him

by mistake. On the way, he'll unwrap one
or two pieces of chocolate and set them on his tongue,
let them melt slow and delicious as any pleasure
he's ever denied himself or been denied.

PRACTICING LOVE

Single in a new town, my friend goes
to bars, dim temples of need, and tries
to meet women. On this Sunday night
he whistles over the phone at the sum
of years my marriage totals and tells me
that I practice love while he believes love
only as theory, some divine and abstract truth.
Moments later, recounting the puzzlework
of hooks and ties that held shut the breath-thin
lingerie his last lover wore, he laughs
and I laugh with him. The two of us
have leaped the gap between theory and practice
and back enough to know time and circumstance,
not fate, dictate the coming close, the falling away
of bodies. Every woman I believed
perfect for me sleeps somewhere else tonight.
The woman sleeping upstairs has practiced
love with me until we sometimes get it right.

FIREWORKS

These winter stars are frozen chips of light,
nothing to gamble the night on, each one wagering
solitude against cold miles of sky. Years before we met,
I stood in a field far from city lights
while a friend mapped each visible constellation.
Because I could not understand anything so enduring,
I forgot each one. Now I invent my own:
the Celtic Dancer, Cassandra the Drag Queen,
the Drunken Fisherman, any name that amuses
and fits the moment's arrangement.

Such random pointing recalls
July's fireworks, pale and temporary flowers
spreading their public blooms against the sky,
then falling, the barely visible smoke vines
that trail them illuminated in the next firing.
It was a Fourth of July when our marriage
nearly hit a soggy end, the hiss and thud
of each poorly-timed word raising our fearful stakes.
By dark we were empty vaults, closed in
on the silence collected in the cold nets of stars

just visible over our backyard. In school
we had learned that the surfaces of stars are not stable
but full of explosions, tendrils of burning gas
rising from their oceans and falling back.
And we learned that the life of each star,
unmeasurable in human years, is nonetheless finite.
For days after, we would be as careful
around one another as those men who defuse
land mines, clipping one wire at a time.
Our sodden words hung in the air,

stale as the morning after one of the local celebrations,
cups of flat beer turning brown
with the cigarettes drowned in them, the ashes danced
into the carpet, raw odor of cordite still floating

in our nostrils. We have lasted beyond
even our most spectacular explosions.
That night I walked to see the fireworks
we had planned to watch together.
In some yards, kids and the not-so-young
twirled sparklers, groaned at or cheered

the fizzle or burst of Roman candles,
ran coughing from smoke bombs. At the fairgrounds,
the crowd's huge voice raised at each outbreak
of colored fire, gaudy coins flung across night's table
to be lost. In the aftermath of that proud
and fragile display, dull echoes
of our afternoon words rocked in my chest.
Small explosions still bit night's edges,
but the presiding fire of stars swam back in view,
and my only thought was to get home to you.

What We Will Not Drown In

If enough water is not falling
between us to fill an ocean,
there's certainly enough to raise
the curving brown river you sleep beside
tonight. I imagine that house
where you and your friends have gone
to flee jobs, husbands, children this weekend
blooming with white and gold light.
Once you might have imagined me
in the noir-light of the street
that works past coffeeshops and clubs,
each catering to a different hunger.
But it's just me and whatever light rises
out of this rectangle of paper tonight.
The rain that spangles these windows
makes every distant reflection
an asymmetrical bloom, a drowning flower.
Earlier tonight, a sudden storm caught me
exiting the grocery store. I pressed
my back against the brick storefront
as rain multiplied the distance
to the car. A row of people lined beside me
like ducks in a carnival gallery;
every now and then one made
a hunched-over high-stepping run
into the parking lot. I'm thinking now
how like them we were
the first time we met. We looked at each other
and saw a storm that would not pass.
So we shook our heads and stepped right in it.

After Weather

Summer is a fierce kiss that comes too soon
and asks too much, a hot mouth that banishes
the shy courtships and flirtations of spring.

To escape the stifled house, the palms of sweat
that settle on us the minute we cease moving,
I erase each day's last suffocating hour

by watering the front yard we hacked clear of grass
and seeded with wildflowers. Soon, we hope,
our lot will be a cool assault, a seduction, of color,

but now we have only broken dirt, the stray
and arrogant spears of grass. Puddles silver
under the hose's spray and blot into the black earth

the instant I turn the hose in another direction.
Thick clouds hover over a tree line just beginning
to erase itself in dusk. You come outside

to tell me that the forecast is for a night of storms.
A quick wind sweeps out of the top branches;
the first fat drops slap the ground. But I'm lost

in my charade of rain and will not come in.
It is one wisdom of our troubled
and manic time that we may all be taken

in a rush of light so powerful we might
scar rocks with our shadows even as we are
dissolved. But an equal chance says we may not.

If we are not, and if I should precede you
into that storm no one walks out of,
love, remember me like this: a man

watering flowers in the rain, trying to coax
a small beauty out of ground he has torn
and laughing at how our best gestures
lose themselves in simple turns of weather.

THE OTHER SIDE OF SLEEP

When her voice breaks out of her throat
and fractures the thin vessel of my sleep,
when she moans, caught
in the web of what lies beneath our waking,
then I must reach her with my hand,
must speak human words until she surfaces.

And when she has calmed, has risen
to stand in the shadow-dispelling light
of the bathroom and sip a glass of water
slow as medicine, when she has settled
back into sleep, her breath once more easy
and regular as a child's bedtime story,
then I am left trying to name
what lies at the bottom of our sleep.

Only twice has my own fear wakened me
from a dream. And perhaps it is some measure
of how far the brain will go to deny
what lives inside it when I confess
that I cannot recall what chased me
those fevered nights. The window sleep opens

is a single eye that peers down on a river
constant as our breathing. Night after night,
we close our eyes and sink our day-worn bodies
into those waters, hoping not to stir
the life in that silty water,
that ancestor whose shape we do not know
but recognize as our own.

THE LANGUAGE OF BIRDS

What does the river say to a woman
sleeping beneath a window left open
so she can hear its murmur and roll all night?
With first light, migrations of birds
will rise out of damp tatters of grass
to fill the empty tent sky raises over water.

The birds do not know the river's name,
do not spend hours, as she does, watching
its topography. They only know the blood-urge
lifting them into flight, the compass guiding them
down the wide alley of water. And the woman
sleeping below them is filled

with the language of birds,
her limbs weaving patterns of flight
as if she might rise at any moment
from the ropy nest of sheets, as if this house,
the car that ferries her to a job
she endures, the little square of garden

she turns anew each spring,
mattock blade lifting like a wing
to bury itself in damp soil,
all could be erased if the next motion
might discover her in flight.
Once or twice a week, after work, she drives

to a bar to drink and watch day smolder,
bed of burning feathers, the deep, temporary red
a glaring screen across the window. Sometimes she takes home
a man with the air of other places about him.
In bed, most of them are quick and clumsy,
as if they do not trust her not to vanish.

In the morning, the river looks wider,
less passable than before, each of them
shuffling through farewells rehearsed

since their bodies rolled apart. Still,
she dreams of the one whose hand
will awaken upon her, will translate flight

into the world of flesh that is also
the world of disappointment. Only in sleep
does she progress toward the invisible
places birds and rivers know.
Once, at dawn, she startled a gray water bird
out of the high weeds whiskering the bank.

Its wings wide as any man's span,
it rose with the slow assurance
of one who carries his destination
wherever he goes, who knows
that any resting place is temporary,
no matter what name it is given.

Happy Endings

The closer we get to the story's end,
the less we believe them.
The prince never arrives in time
to kiss the drugged apple
from the mouth of the princess.
We come to savor the litter of bodies
spread over the stage at the play's end,
want to rise and call after the lovers
who stroll happily away: *No.*
You'll age and not gracefully.
You'll wake after midnight and feel
your heart gnawed by every wrong choice
you've made.
Outside the wide front window
of the public library's reading room, I watched a girl
barely in her teens try to hide her easy tears
as she hung up the pay phone. Her friends
flocked around her, surrounded her
with the bodies they were just beginning
to wear with some grace. They were not so far away
from believing *and they lived happily ever after,*
the story-teller's lie that means good night,
that says if we live through one great trial,
then our lives will settle into some sure
and plotless groove. We never tell children
how the story continues:
the morning after
the wedding, the prince and princess wake,
stale-mouthed and grouchy from the ride,
the wedding feast and too much wine.
And for the rest of her days in the castle,
the ones no stories are woven from,
she will pause when she hears the tuneless
rhythm of shovels, the droning song of the workers
so much like that of the peasants

who sheltered her when she fled the kingdom,
the ones she never looked back to see
when the prince took her away.
                              Still,
if we can tell a story in which any lovers
find some grace, we should believe any happiness
we can contrive. Hear me, little one,
you with your tears drying and your head
turning to sleep, all stories end,
most of them unhappily, but we can never cease
telling them, can never surrender the hope
lying at the bottom of the page.